UKULELE

LOVE BALLADS

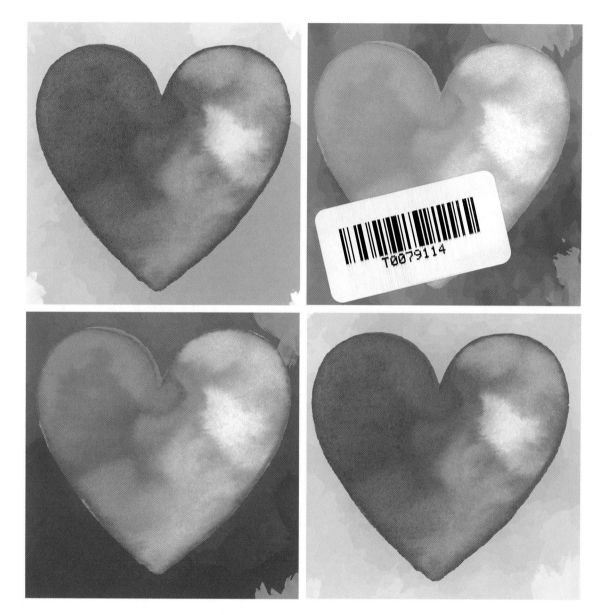

ISBN 978-1-5400-7038-8

HAL•LEONARD®

Visit Hal Leonard Online at
www.halleonard.com

Contact us:
Hal Leonard
7777 West Bluemound Road
Milwaukee, WI 53213
Email: info@halleonard.com

In Europe, contact:
Hal Leonard Europe Limited
42 Wigmore Street
Marylebone, London, W1U 2RN
Email: info@halleonardeurope.com

In Australia, contact:
Hal Leonard Australia Pty. Ltd.
4 Lentara Court
Cheltenham, Victoria, 3192 Australia
Email: info@halleonard.com.au

CONTENTS

All of Me

Words and Music by John Stephens and Toby Gad

mag - i - cal mys - ter - y ride. _____ And I'm
- tion, my rhy - thm and blues. _____ I can't stop

so diz - zy; don't know what hit me, but I'll be all
sing - in', ___ it's ring - in' in _____ my head ___ for you. _

Pre-Chorus

right. }
___ My head's un - der wa - ter, _____ but I'm _

_____ breath - ing fine. _____ You're _ cra - zy and I'm _

_____ out _ of my mind. _____ 'Cause

ning.   'Cause I give you all _____ of me, _

_____   and you give me all _____

To Coda ⊕ |1.

_____ of   you, ___   oh. _____

|2.

___   oh. _____   Give   me   all _____ of   you. _

Bridge
Gm   F

_____ Cards   on ___ the ta - ble, ___ we're both _

show - ing hearts. ___ Risk - ing ___ it all, ___

D.S. al Coda

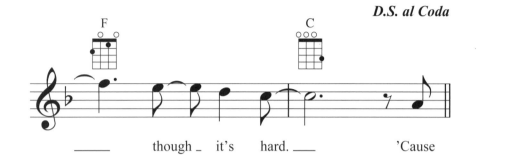

though _ it's hard. ___ 'Cause ___

Outro

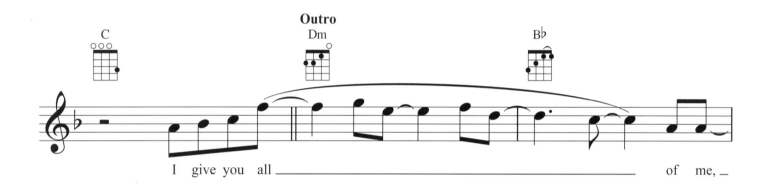

I give you all _____ of me, _

and you give me all _____

of you, ___ oh. _____

Evermore

from BEAUTY AND THE BEAST
Music by Alan Menken
Lyrics by Tim Rice

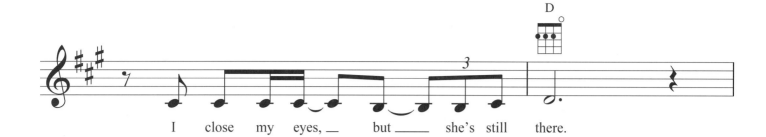

I close my eyes, __ but __ she's still there.

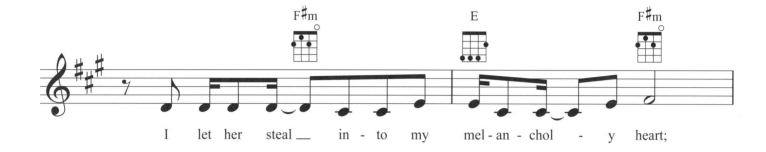

I let her steal __ in-to my mel-an-chol - y heart;

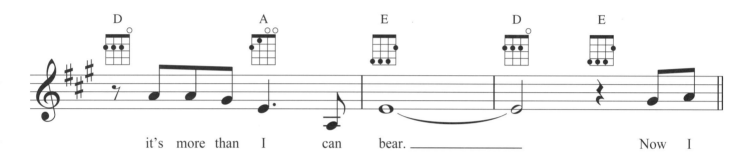

it's more than I can bear. _____ Now I

Chorus

know she'll nev - er leave me, e - ven as she runs a -

way. She will still tor - ment __ me, calm me, hurt __ me, move __

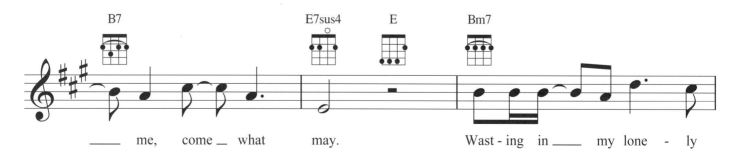

__ me, come __ what may. Wast - ing in __ my lone - ly

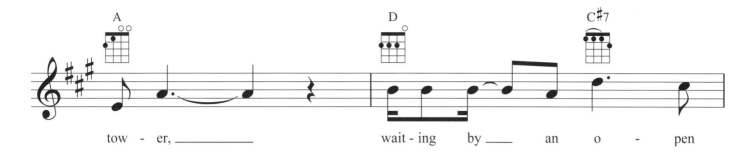

tow - er, _____ wait - ing by ___ an o - pen

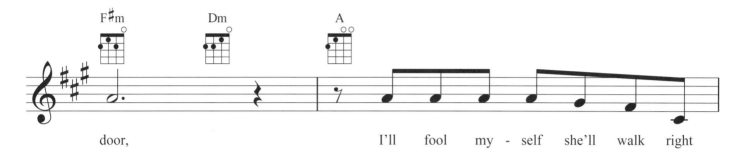

door, I'll fool my - self she'll walk right

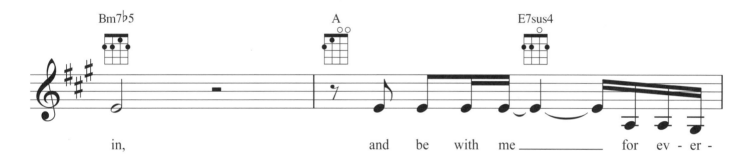

in, and be with me _____ for - ev - er -

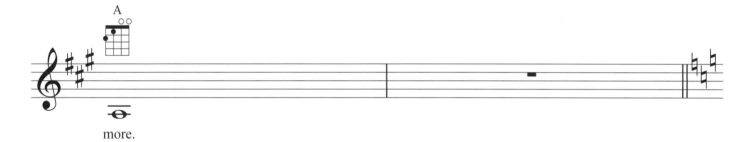

more.

Verse

2. I rage a - gainst ___ the trials of love.

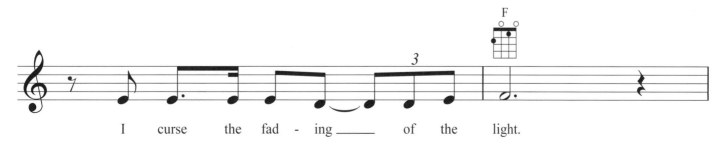

I curse the fad - ing _____ of the light.

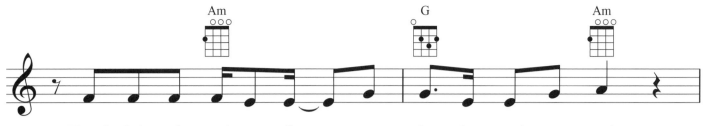

Though she's al - read - y flown __ so far be - yond my reach,

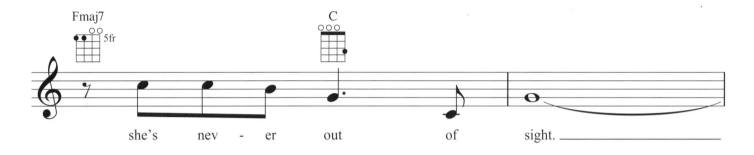

she's nev - er out of sight. _____

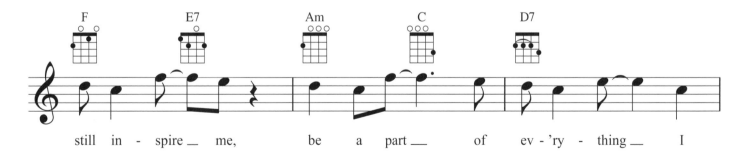

Chorus

__ Now I know she'll nev - er

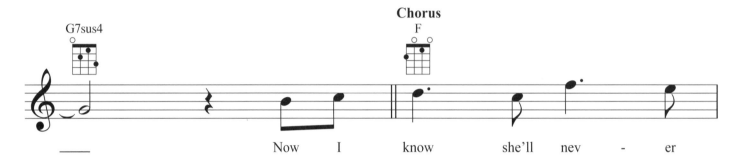

leave me, e - ven as she fades from view. She will

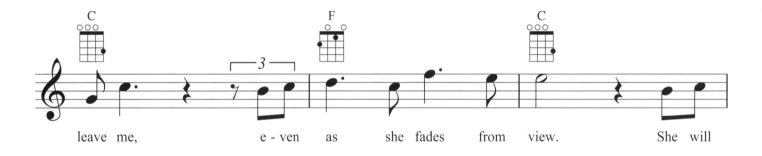

still in - spire __ me, be a part __ of ev - 'ry - thing __ I

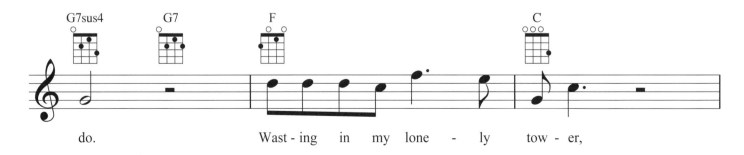

do. Wast - ing in my lone - ly tow - er,

Beautiful Crazy

Words and Music by Robert Williford, Luke Combs and Wyatt Durrette

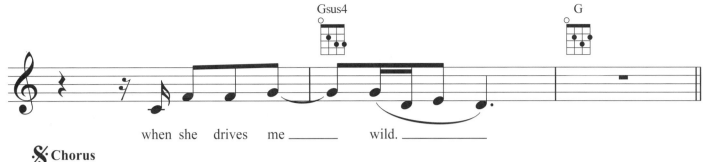

when she drives me _____ wild. _____

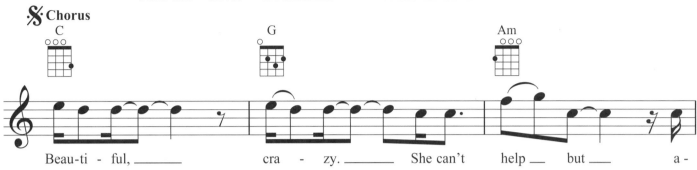

Chorus

Beau-ti-ful, _____ cra - zy. _____ She can't help _ but _ a -

maze me, _____ the way that she danc - es, ain't a - fraid to take chanc - es, and

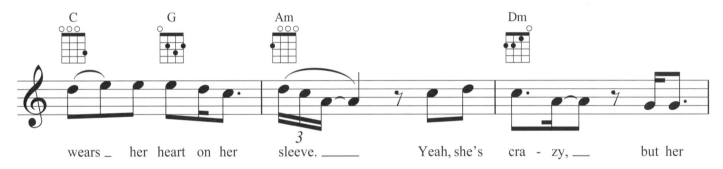

wears _ her heart on her sleeve. _____ Yeah, she's cra - zy, __ but her

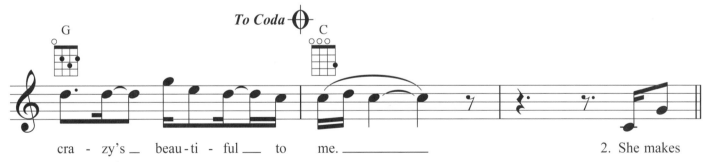

To Coda

cra - zy's _ beau - ti - ful __ to me. _____ 2. She makes

Verse

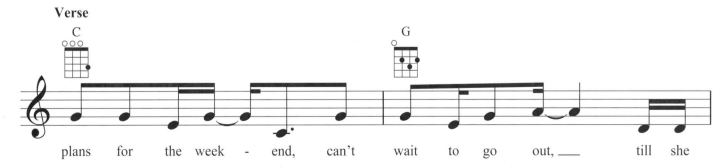

plans for the week - end, can't wait to go out, ___ till she

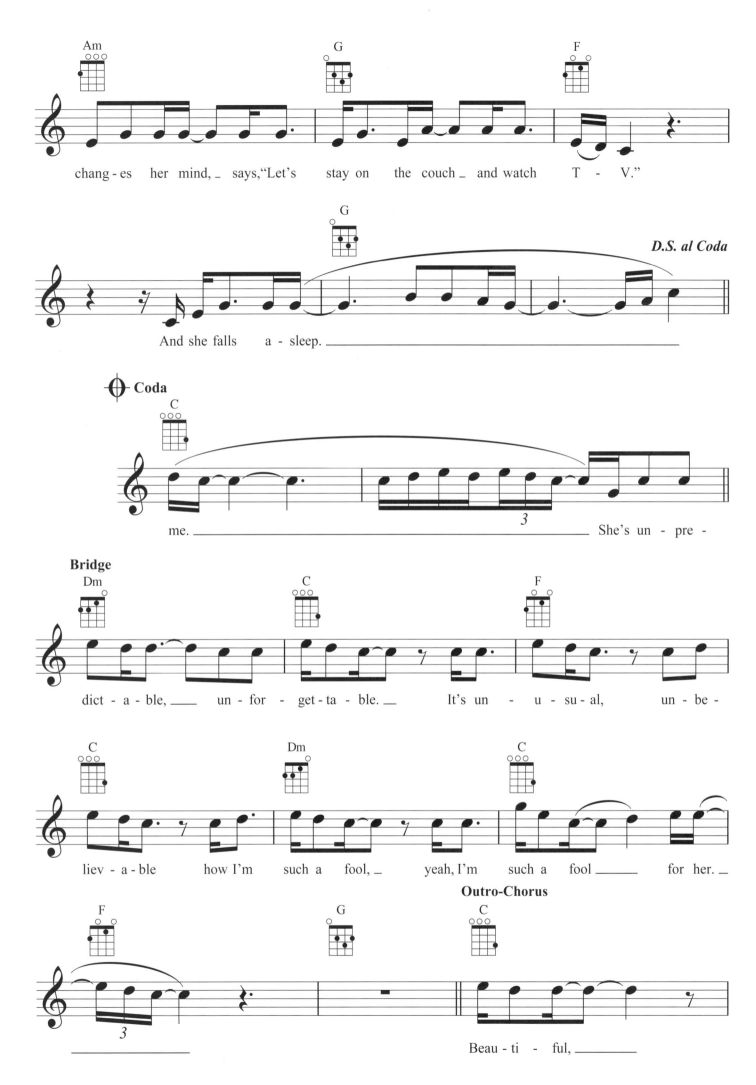

changes her mind, _ says, "Let's stay on the couch _ and watch T - V."

D.S. al Coda

And she falls a - sleep. _____

Coda

me. _____ She's un - pre -

Bridge

dict - a - ble, _____ un - for - get - ta - ble. _ It's un - u - su - al, un - be -

liev - a - ble how I'm such a fool, _ yeah, I'm such a fool _____ for her.

Outro-Chorus

Beau - ti - ful, _____

cra - zy. _____ She can't help but __ a - maze me, _____ the

way that she danc - es, ain't a - fraid to take chanc - es, and

wears her heart on her sleeve. _____ Yeah, she's cra - zy, __ ah, she's

cra - zy, _____ she's cra - zy, __ but her cra - zy's __ beau - ti - ful __ to

me. _____ Her

cra - zy's __ beau - ti - ful __ to me.

Best Part of Me

Words and Music by Ed Sheeran, Benjamin Levin and Abbey Smith

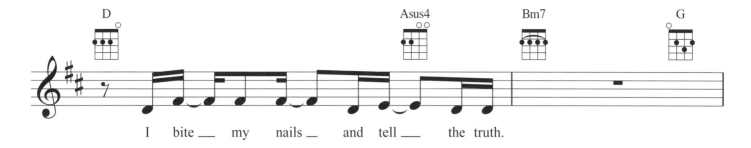

I bite __ my nails __ and tell __ the truth.

I go __ from thin __ to o - ver-weight; __ day __ to day __ it fluc - tu - ates. __

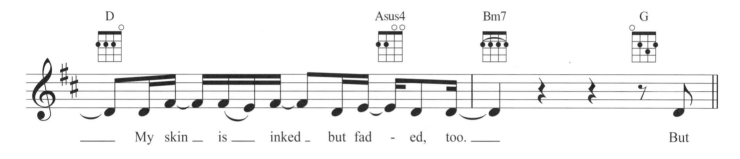

__ My skin __ is __ inked __ but fad - ed, too. __ But

Pre-Chorus

she loves __ me, she loves __ me. Why __ the hell __ d'she love __ me

when she could have an - y - one __ else? __ Oh,

you love __ me, you love __ me. Why __ the hell __ d'you love __ me?

And I nev - er catch _ the train _ on time, __ al-ways thir - ty min - utes be-hind. _

___ Your _ wor-ries ain't _ seen __ noth-ing ___ yet. But

Pre-Chorus

you love _ me, you love _ me. Why the hell __ d'you love _ me so _

when you could have an - y - one ___ else? ___ Yeah, ___

he loves _ me, he loves _ me, and I bet he nev - er lets _ me go

and shows me how _ to love _ my - self. *Both:* 'Cause,

Chorus

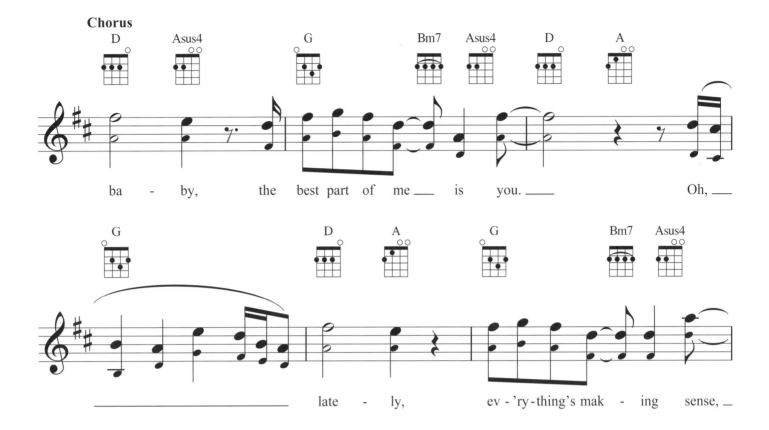

ba - by, the best part of me ___ is you. ___ Oh, ___

lately, ev -'ry-thing's mak - ing sense, ___

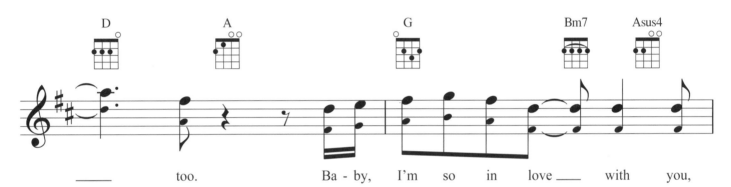

___ too. Ba - by, I'm so in love ___ with you,

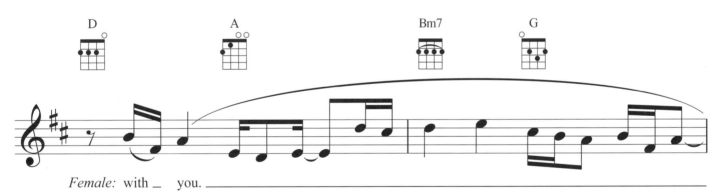

Female: with ___ you. ___

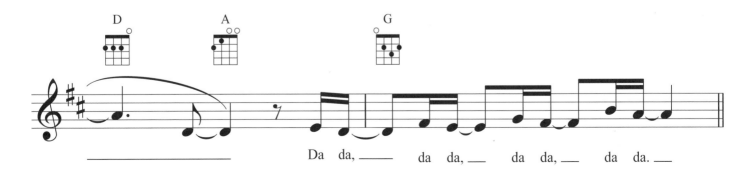

___ Da da, ___ da da, ___ da da, ___ da da. ___

22

Have I Told You Lately

Words and Music by Van Morrison

Outro

told you there's no one else a - bove you? You fill my heart with glad-ness,

take a - way __ my sad - ness, ease my trou-bles, that's __ what you

do. Take a - way all ___ my sad - ness,

fill my life with glad- ness, ease my trou-bles, that's _ what you do.

Take a - way all ___ my sad - ness, fill my heart with glad __ ness,

ease my trou - bles, that's __ what you do. _____

Heaven

Words and Music by Bryan Adams and Jim Vallance

Bb   F   Gsus4   G

o-ver now. ___
hold me now, ___

You keep me comin' back for more. ___
'cause our ___ love will light the way. ___

𝄋 **Chorus**

F   G   Am   C   F

Ba-by, you're all ___ that I want   when you're ly-in' here ___ in my arms.   I'm

G   Am   G

find-ing it hard ___ to be-lieve   we're in heav-en.   And

F   G   Am   C   F

love is all ___ that I need,   and I found it there ___ in your heart.   It

To Coda ⊕ 1. G

is-n't too hard ___ to see ___   we're in heav-en.

C   Am   C   Fadd9

(Instrumental)

28

Just the Way You Are

Words and Music by Billy Joel

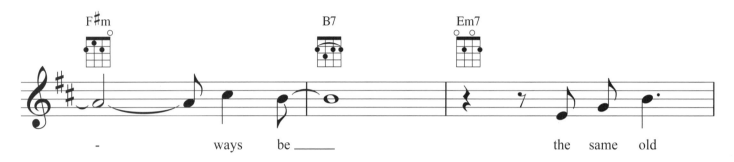

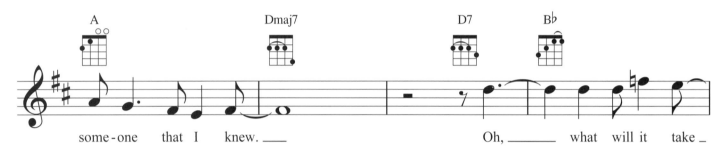

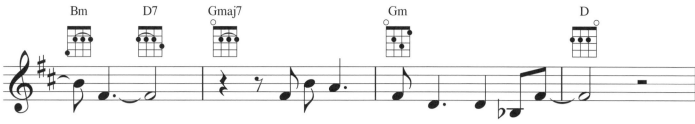

-er, _____ and this I prom - ise from the heart. _____

Mm. _____ I could not love _____ you _____ an - y bet -

- ter; I love _ you just _____ the way _____ you are. _

D.S. al Coda
(Lyric 2)

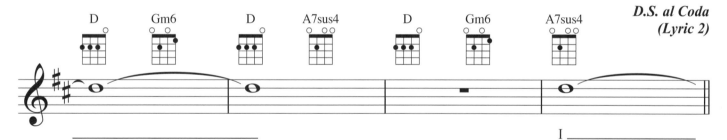

_____ I _____

Outro

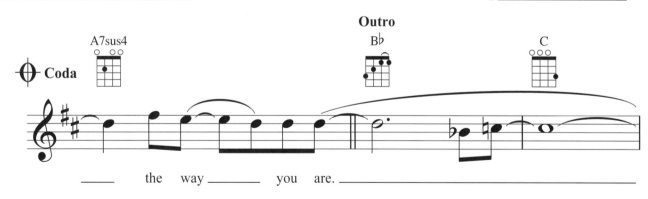

_____ the way _____ you are. _____

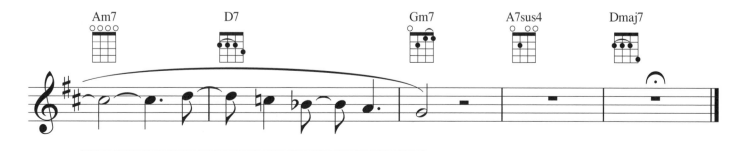

Love Someone

Words and Music by Lukas Forchhammer, Morten Ristorp, Morten Pilegaard, Jaramye Daniels, Don Stefano, David LaBrel and James Ghaleb

All my life, _____ I thought it'd be

hard to find __ the one till I _____ found you. _____ And I find it

bit - ter - sweet _____ 'cause you

gave me some - thing to lose. _____ But when you

loved some - one ___ like I do. _____ You prob-'ly nev - er

loved some - one _____ like I _____ do. _____

I'll Never Love Again

from A STAR IS BORN

Words and Music by Stefani Germanotta, Aaron Raitiere, Hillary Lindsey and Natalie Hemby

First note

Verse
Moderately slow, in 2

G ... *Em7*

Wish I could, I could-'ve said _ good - bye. ____

Cmaj7

I would-'ve said what I want-ed to, ____ may-be e-ven

D7sus4 ... *G*

cried for you. If I knew ____

Em7

it would be the last time, ____ I would-'ve broke my heart in

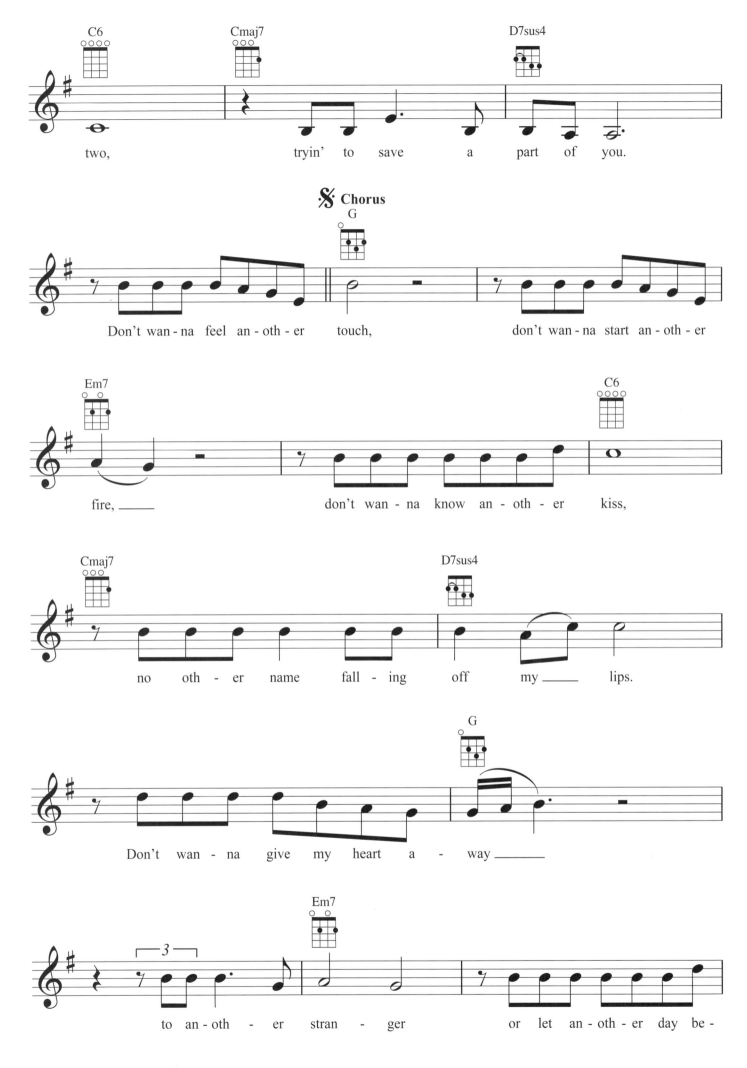

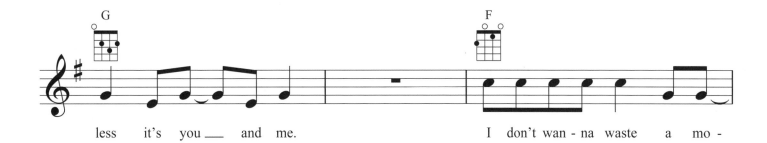

less it's you ___ and me.   I don't wan-na waste a mo-

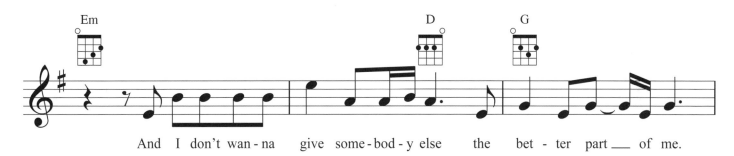

- ment,   ooh. _____

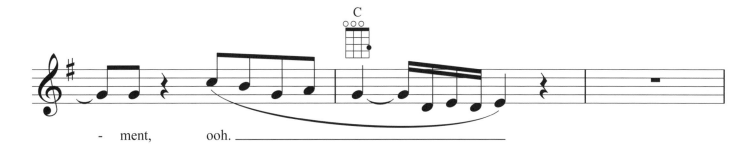

And I don't wan-na give some-bod-y else the bet-ter part ___ of me.

I would rath-er wait for you, ____   ooh. _____

___   Don't wan-na

Chorus

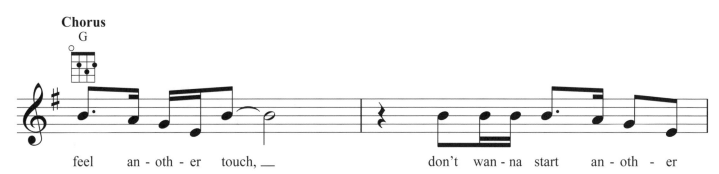

feel an-oth-er touch, ___   don't wan-na start an-oth-er

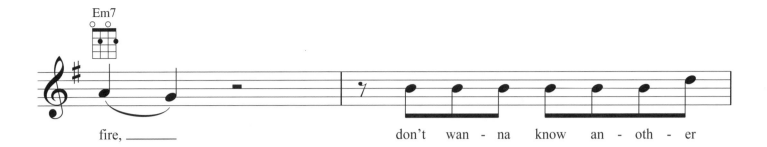

fire, _____

don't wan - na know an - oth - er

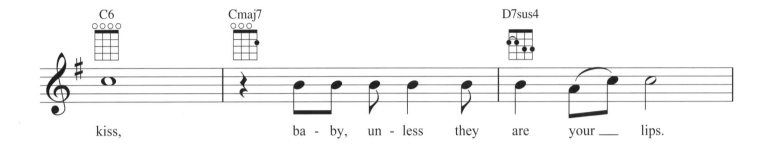

kiss,

ba - by, un - less they are your __ lips.

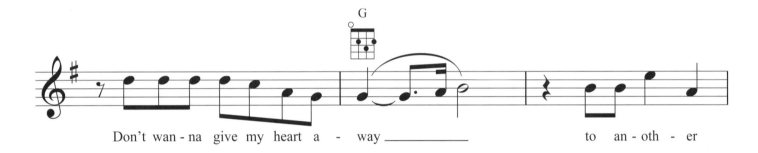

Don't wan - na give my heart a - way _____ to an - oth - er

stran - ger

or let an - oth - er day be - gin.

Won't

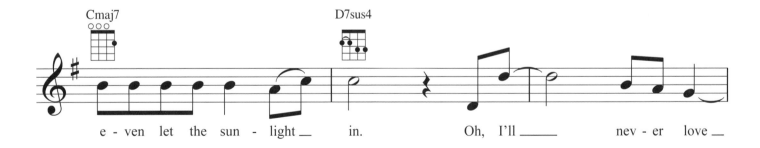

e - ven let the sun - light __ in.

Oh, I'll _____ nev - er love __

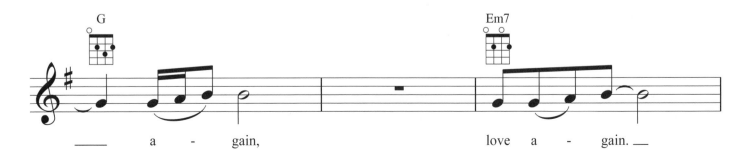

____ a - gain,

love a - gain. __

42

Never Enough

from THE GREATEST SHOWMAN
Words and Music by Benj Pasek and Justin Paul

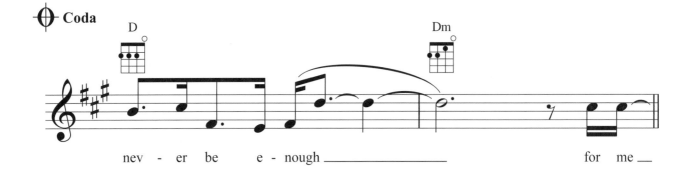

Coda

never be e-nough _____ for me _____

Outro

_____ Nev-er, nev-er Nev-er, nev-er Nev-er, for me, _____

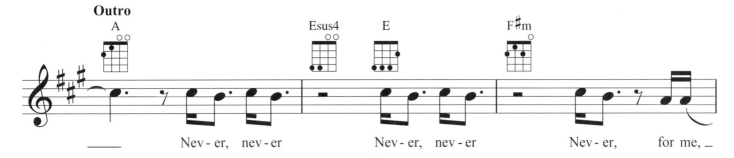

_____ for me _____ Nev-er e-nough, _____ nev-er, nev-er

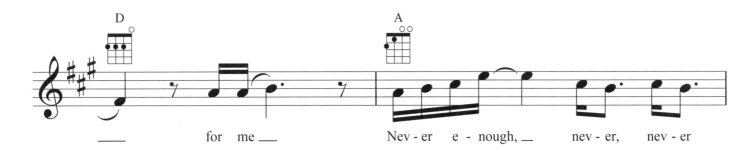

Nev-er e-nough, _____ nev-er, nev-er Nev-er e-nough _____ for me, _____

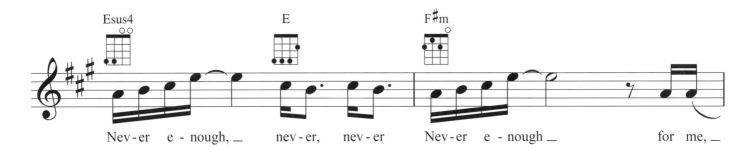

_____ for me, _____ for me, _____

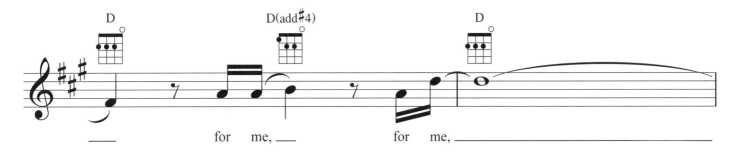

Freely

_____ for me _____

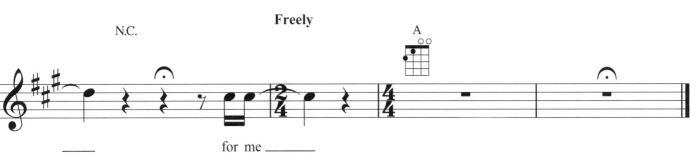

Lover

Words and Music by Taylor Swift

D.S. al Coda

This is our place; we make the call. ___ I'm

high-ly sus-pi-cious that ev-'ry-one who sees you wants ___ you. ___ I've

loved you three sum-mers now, hon-ey, but I want 'em all. ___ Can

Coda
Bridge

La-dies and gen-tle-men, will you please stand?

With ev-'ry gui-tar string scar on my hand,

Outro-Chorus

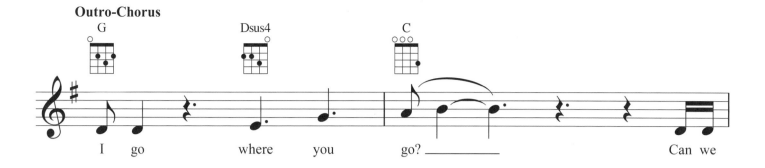

I go where you go? _____ Can we

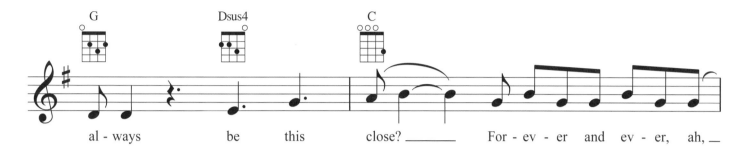

al - ways be this close? _____ For - ev - er and ev - er, ah, __

_____ take me out and take me home. _ You're

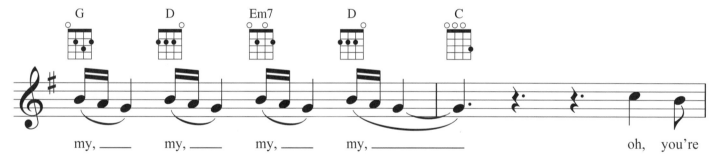

my, ___ my, ___ my, ___ my, _____ oh, you're

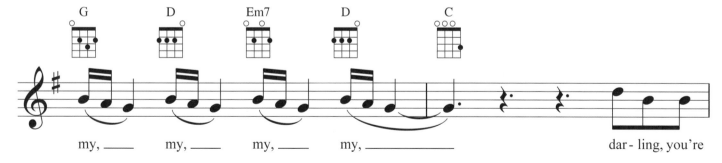

my, ___ my, ___ my, ___ my, _____ dar - ling, you're

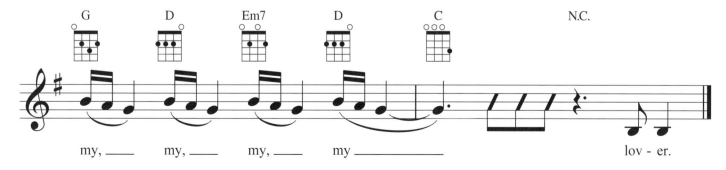

my, ___ my, ___ my, ___ my _____ lov - er.

Perfect

Words and Music by Ed Sheeran

time. _____ Dar - ling, just kiss me slow, your heart is
time. _____ Dar - ling, just hold my hand. Be my girl, I'll

all ___ I ___ own. And in your eyes, you're ___ hold - ing mine. _
be ___ your ___ man. I've seen the fu - ture ___ in your eyes. _

Chorus

___ } Ba - by, _____ I'm danc - ing in the

dark with you be - tween my arms. Bare - foot on the

grass, lis - ten - ing to our ___ fa - v'rite song. { When you said you looked a
                                                     { When I saw you in that

To Coda ⊕

mess, I whis - pered un - der - neath my breath. But you heard it, "Dar - ling,
dress, look - ing so beau - ti - ful, I don't ___ de - serve this. "Dar - ling,

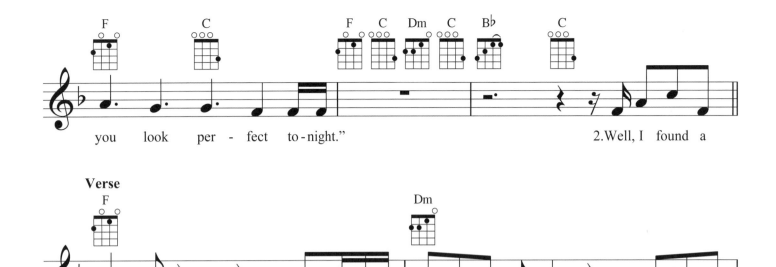

you look per-fect to-night." 2.Well, I found a

Verse

wom-an, strong-er than an - y-one I know. She shares my

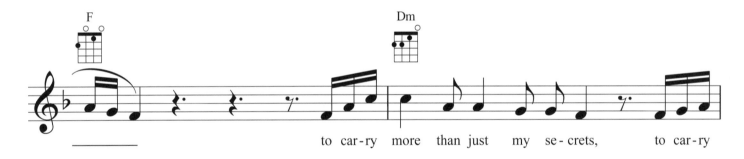

dreams; I hope __ that some-day I'll share her home. _____ I found a love __

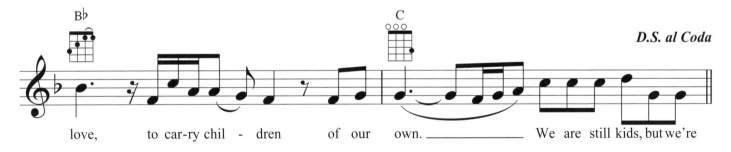

_____ to car-ry more than just my se-crets, to car-ry

D.S. al Coda

love, to car-ry chil - dren of our own. _____ We are still kids, but we're

Interlude

Coda

you look per - fect to-night."

Outro-Chorus

Ba - by, _____ I'm _____ danc - ing in the

dark with you be - tween my arms. Bare - foot on the

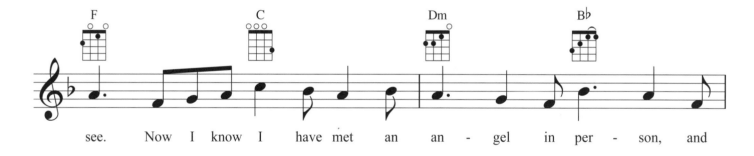

grass, lis - ten - ing to our ___ fa - v'rite song. I have faith in what _ I

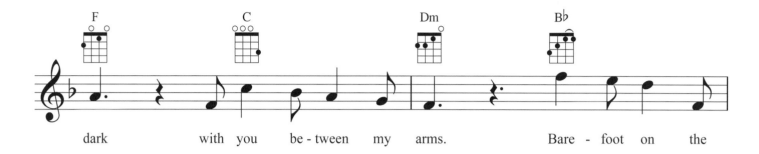

see. Now I know I have met an an - gel in per - son, and

she looks per - fect. I don't de - serve this, you look per - fect to - night.

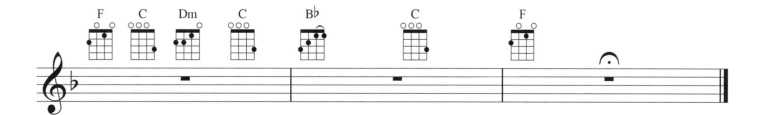

Remedy

Words and Music by Adele Adkins and Ryan Tedder

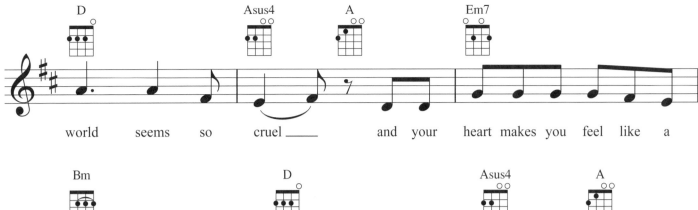

world   seems   so   cruel ____   and   your   heart makes you feel like a

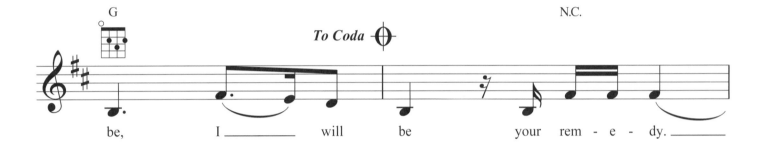

fool, ____   I   prom - ise   you __ will   see __   that I _____ will

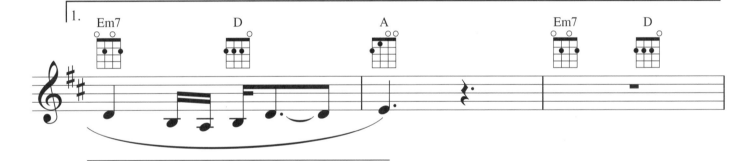

be,   I _____ will   be   your   rem - e - dy. ____

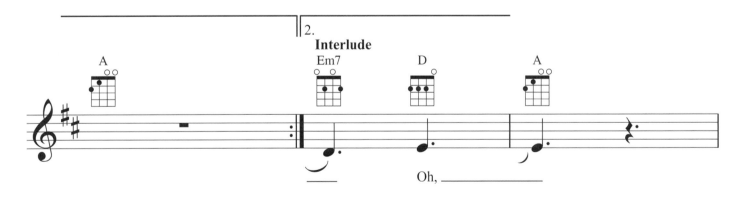

____   Oh, _____

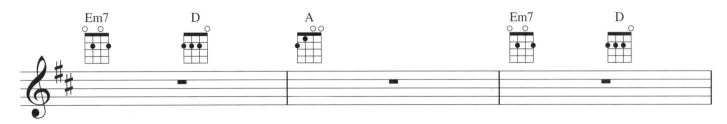

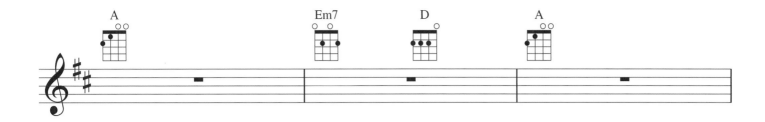

D.S. al Coda

When the

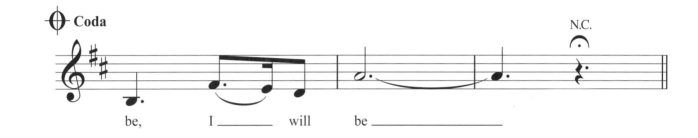

Coda

N.C.

be,   I _____ will   be _____

Outro

your rem - e - dy. _____

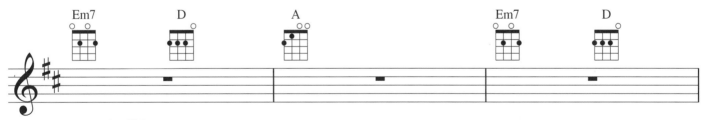

Vocal ad lib.

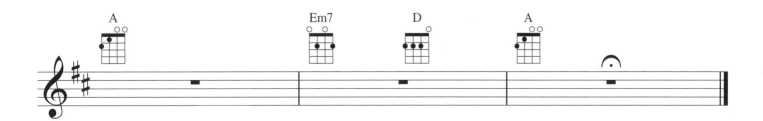

Right Here Waiting

Words and Music by Richard Marx

1. O-ceans a-part, _____ day af-ter day, _____ and I
2. I took for grant - ed all the times _____ that I

slow - ly go _____ in - sane. _____ I hear your voice _____ on the line, _____
thought would last _____ some - how. _____ I hear the laugh - ter, I taste the tears, _

_____ but it does - n't stop _____ the pain. If I see you next _
_____ but I can't get near _____ you now. Oh, can't you see _

_____ to nev - er, _____ how can we say _____ for - ev - er? _____
_____ it, ba - by? _____ You've got me go - in' cra - zy. _____

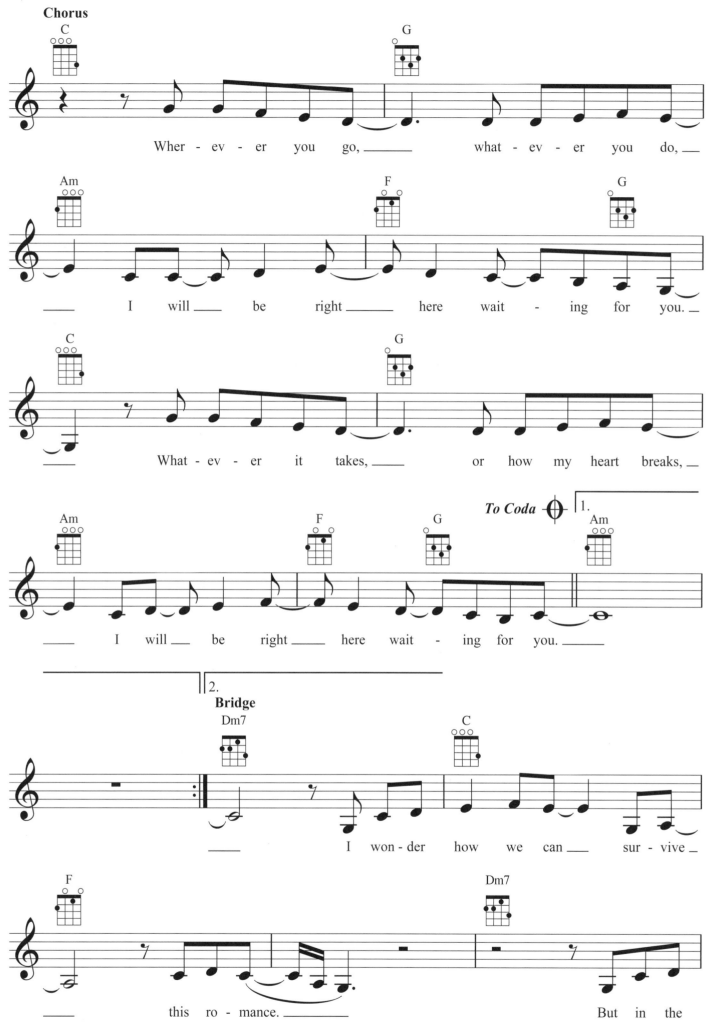

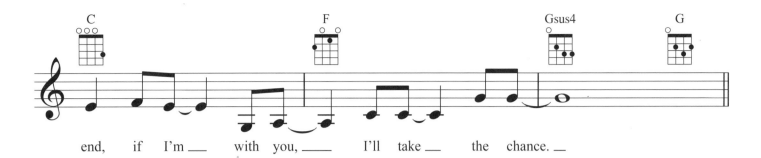

end, if I'm ___ with you, ___ I'll take ___ the chance. ___

Interlude

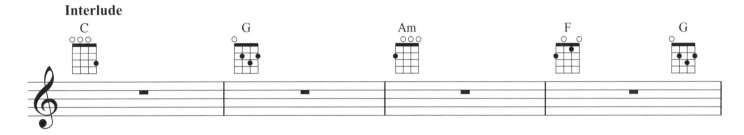

D.S. al Coda
(Lyric 2)

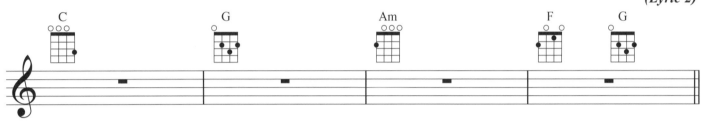

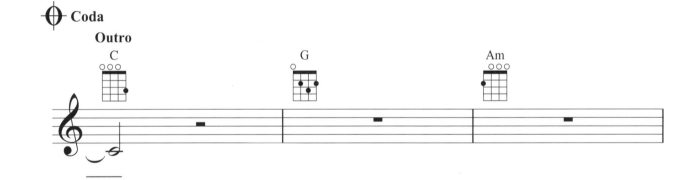

Coda

Outro

Wait - ing for you. _____

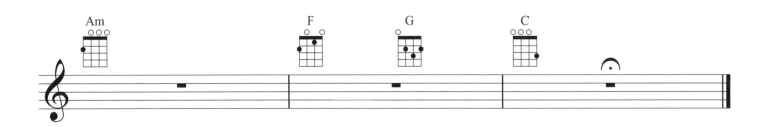

Someone You Loved

Words and Music by Lewis Capaldi, Benjamin Kohn,
Peter Kelleher, Thomas Barnes and Samuel Roman

Say You Won't Let Go

Words and Music by Steven Solomon, James Arthur and Neil Ormandy

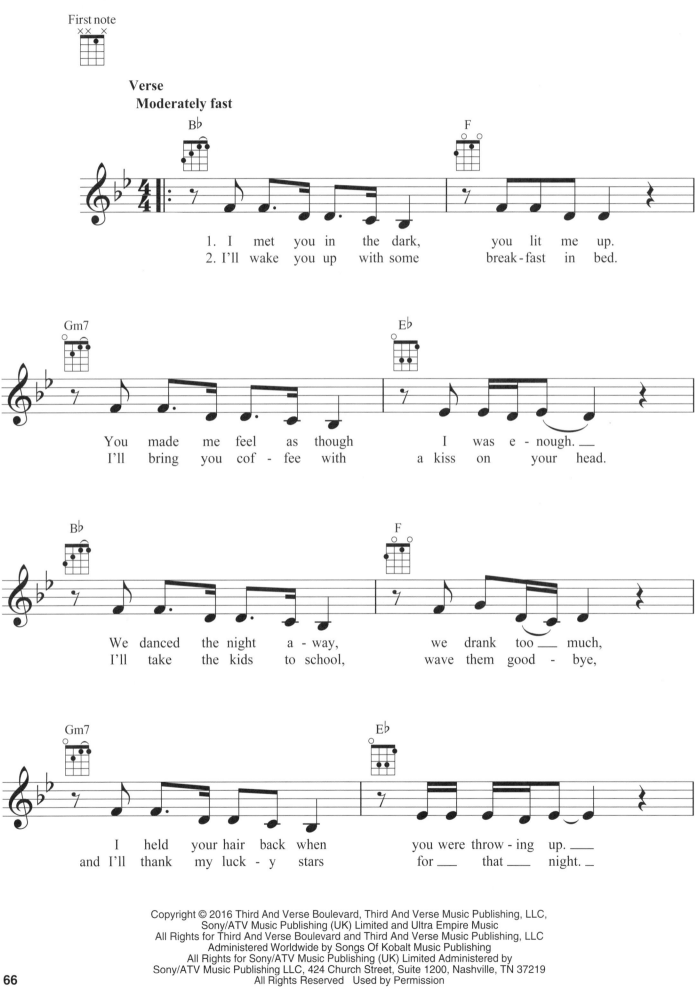

Then you smiled o - ver your shoul - der. For a min - ute, I was stone - cold so - ber.
When you looked o - ver your shoul - der, for a min - ute, I'll for - get that I'm old - er.

I pulled you clos - er to my _____ chest.
I wan - na dance with you right _____ now.

And you asked me to stay o - ver. I said, "I al - read - y told ya
And you look as beau - ti - ful as ev - er, and I swear that ev - 'ry day you'll get bet - ter.

I think that you should get some _____ rest."
You make me feel this way some - how.

Pre-Chorus

I knew I loved you then, but you'd nev - er know,
I'm so in love with you, and I hope you know,
I'm gon - na love you till my lungs give out.

Speechless

Words and Music by Dan Smyers, Shay Mooney, Jordan Reynolds and Laura Veltz

I've been in a daze ev - er since the day that we met.

You take the breath out of my lungs, can't e - ven fight it,

and all of the words out of my mouth with - out e - ven try - in'. And

D.S. al Coda

I'm

Interlude

Coda

speech- less.

Pre-Chorus

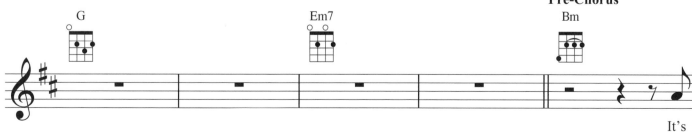

It's

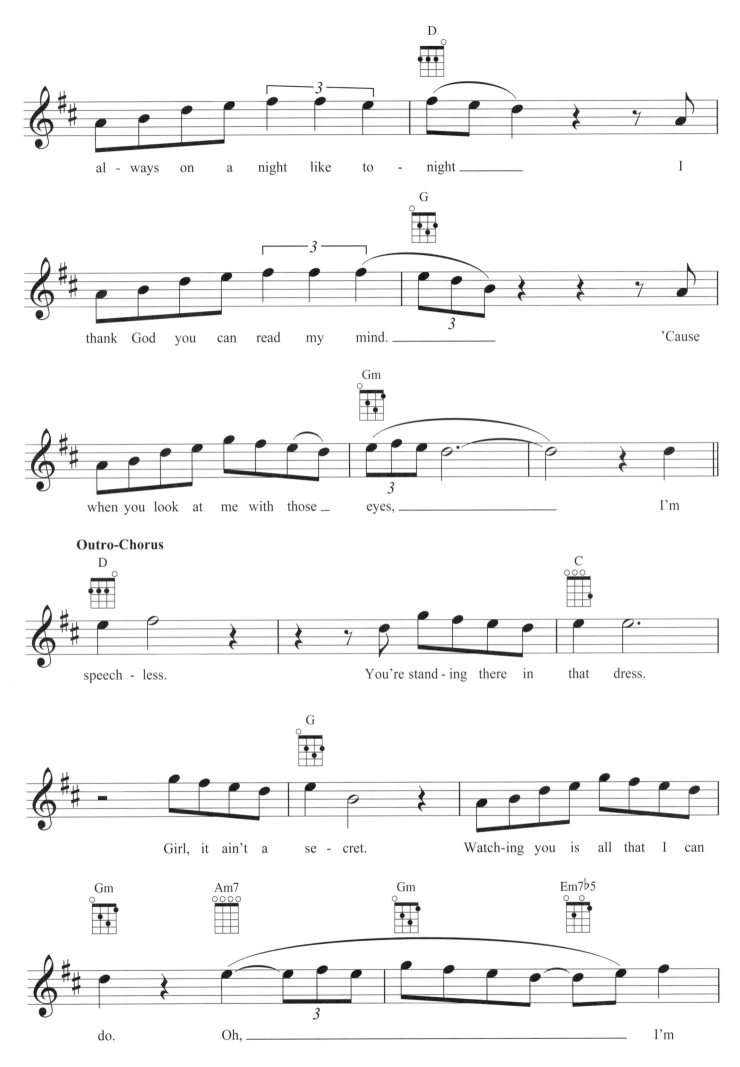

al - ways on a night like to - night _____ I

thank God you can read my mind. _____ 'Cause

when you look at me with those _ eyes, _____ I'm

Outro-Chorus

speech - less. You're stand - ing there in that dress.

Girl, it ain't a se - cret. Watch - ing you is all that I can

do. Oh, _____ I'm

A Thousand Years

from the Summit Entertainment film THE TWILIGHT SAGA: BREAKING DAWN – PART 1

Words and Music by David Hodges and Christina Perri

doubt _____ sud - den - ly _____ goes a - way some -
breath, _____ ev - er - y _____ hour has ___ come to _____

how. }
this: }   One   step   clos -

Chorus 1

- er. _____   I have died __ ev - 'ry day, __

wait - ing for _____ you.   Dar - ling, don't __ be a - fraid. __

I have loved __ you for a thou - sand years, _____ I'll

1.

love you for ___ a thou - sand   more. _____

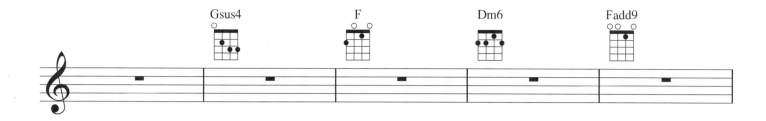

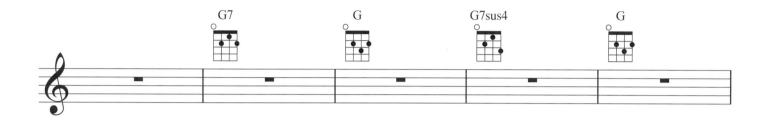

Pre-Chorus

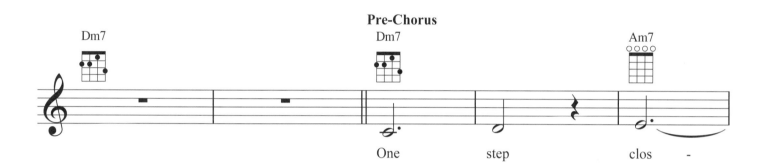

One step clos -

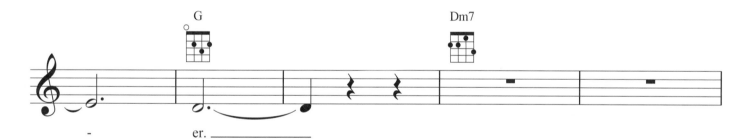

- er.

One step clos - er.

D.S. al Coda
(take 2nd ending)

Coda

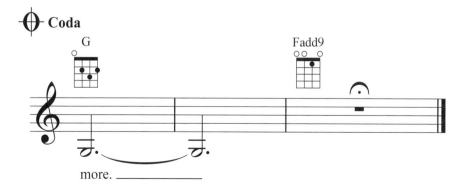

more.

You Are the Reason

Words and Music by Calum Scott, Corey Sanders and Jonathan Maguire

Bridge

son. I don't wan-na fight no more. I don't wan-na hide no more.

I don't wan-na cry no more. Come back; I need __ you to hold __

__ me a lit-tle clos-er now, just a lit-tle clos-er now.

Come a lit-tle clos-er; I need you to hold __ me to-night. __

D.S. al Coda 2

__ I'd climb ev-'ry

Coda 2

that you are the rea - son. __

Your Song

Words and Music by Elton John and Bernie Taupin

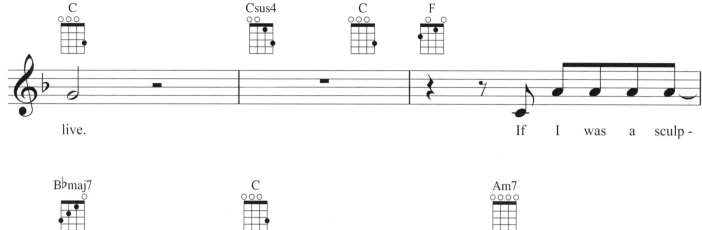

live.   If I was a sculp-

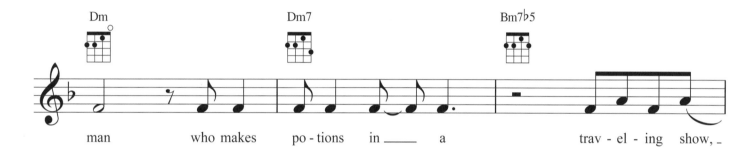

-tor,   but then a-gain, __ no,   or a

man   who makes po-tions in ___ a   trav-el-ing show, _

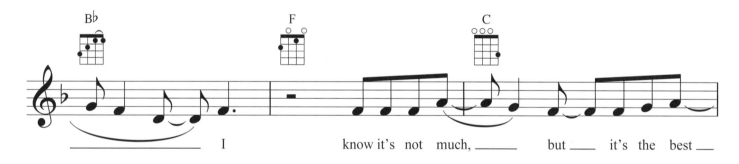

_____ I   know it's not much, _____ but __ it's the best __

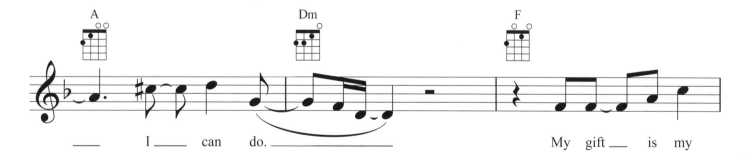

__ I ___ can do. _____   My gift __ is my

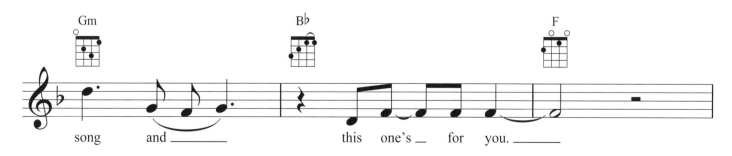

song and _____   this one's _ for you. _____

Additional Lyrics

2. I sat on the roof and kicked off the moss.
   Well a few of the verses, well, they've got me quite cross.
   But the sun's been quite kind while I wrote this song.
   It's for people like you that keep it turned on.

   So excuse me forgetting but these things I do.
   You see, I've forgotten if they're green or they're blue.
   Anyway, the thing is, what I really mean,
   Yours are the sweetest eyes I've ever seen.

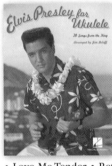